# Assistants
# Virtual

# Assistants Virtual

# **Table Of Contents**

# Foreword

Most businesses today, whether big or small are accepting the idea of having virtual assistance, this lessens the workload on the company and is cheaper than having to create a whole department to take on the same tasks. Virtual assistance is fast becoming a popular option for many. Get all the info you need here.

# *Virtual Assistants*

How to Run a Successful Virtual Assistants Business

# Chapter 1:

*Virtual Assistant Basics*

---

# Synopsis

The following are some reason a business owner may want to consider the advantages virtual assistance brings:

# The Basics

Basically a virtual assistant will be able to carry the work load given simply because of the focused nature of the particular assignments given. In most cases such virtual assistance capabilities are much more refined and thus able to handle the delegated task with ease.

Hiring the services of virtual assistance would effectively mean hiring someone who is an expert in his or her own field.

The need to teach the individual would not be a factor in the equation nor would there be a need to constantly monitor the situation to ensure the desired results are forthcoming.

With the use of virtual assistance the assignments can be done within the time lines, as the reputation of the virtual assistance depends broadly on the ability to produce the work effectively and accurately with the time frame agreed upon.

Virtual assistance platforms can also be trusted to keep the confidentiality of the task at hand because here again the reputation built by the services rendered would be the deciding point of most choices made to hire the particular individual's services.

Effective communication and clear responsibilities outlines for the virtual assistance is enough to get the job done as compared to having the same tasks tackled within the company where there a many other distractions and demands to contend with.

In terms of the cost factor, it is sometimes cheaper to hire the services of virtual assistance and this is one on the reasons that contributes to its popularity.

# Chapter 2:

## *What Skills Are Needed*

---

# Synopsis

Although not everyone can be a virtual assistant, for those interested in doing this as a revenue earning possibility there are some pointers one should be aware of. Having some computer and communication skills that will help to create a complete package for the virtual assistant is important.

# What Is Needed

The following are some basic skills that most virtual assistants are expected to have:

Word processing skills – because a lot of the work involves word processing, such as data entry, typing and other online documentations the word processing knowledge will come in handy.

The level of accuracy is also something that should not be compromised in any way.

Computer skills – the very nature of the job requires the extensive use of the computer thus the need to be computer conversant. Being able to handle the more popular software and applications is also a pre requisite when it comes to available skills.

Strong communication skill – this is also another necessity when it comes to the capabilities listed for virtual assistance. Being able to communicate effectively and accurately both verbally as well as in writing is very important as a lot of the communication needs to be explicit and understood on all levels.

Strong writing skills – the bulk of the work is done through emails and faxes, therefore there is a need to be well versed in writing skills in order to execute the requirements of the job well.

Proof reading material is also something that is expected as part of the job requirements.

Strong management skills – this will come in handy when there is a need to coordinate several different elements at any given time.

These areas may include the advertising aspect, the marketing side and perhaps even the public relations platform of the business.

The general idea is to help the client grow the business entity.

# Chapter 3:

## *Arranging A Work Area*

---

# Synopsis

Taking the virtual assistant business seriously would include having a designated area to work in and this should ideally be without distractions and disturbances.

Trying to simulate and office environment would be ideal but not totally necessary. If the work area is to be within the actual living premise than there is a need to cordon off an area with the explicit intrusions regarding unwelcomed intrusions.

## Your Space

It should be made very clear that intrusions on the work area will not be tolerated, as this could affect any live communications that happen to be conducted.

The important element to ensure is that when the act of business is being conducted it should be done in a professional manner which gives the client the confidence in entrusting the job to the virtual assistant.

The work area would also have to include the very basics equipment to ensure the individual is able to get the job done effectively, quickly and accurately.

These would ideally include a computer with internet access that is strong, a telephone line, and a work station that is fairly decent in size and uncluttered.

The work area should also be designed to be conducive to work in as the quality of the work produced can be affected by the surrounding s and the inability to focus due to the distractions.

If there is any video connection between client and the virtual assistant the working area of the virtual assistant would speak volumes as to the quality of the work the client can expect.

Therefore keeping the area professional looking will give the client the confidence needed to entrust the job to the individual.

If the option is available to rent a small office space for the reason of conducting the virtual assistant business, then the location chosen should be as centralized as possible.

This would help the individual get things done more easily as everything is within accessible distance.

# Chapter 4:

*Decide What Services You Will Offer*

# Synopsis

There is really no limit as to the type of services that can be offered by the virtual assistant; however the services offered should be in line with the expertise of the individual, otherwise the end results of the work produced will not be up to the client's expectations. This will not serve well for the virtual assistant as the job acquired usually come based on recommendations and track records.

# Your Plan

The main idea behind deciding what services to offer would be deciding first if the said services are part of the capabilities of the individual.

Virtual assistants would do well to only offer services along their own individual expertise and knowledge. Should the individual decide to diversify then the effort must be made to ensure the relevant knowledge and style is properly learnt in order to do the job well.

Among the more popular services that can be offered as a virtual assistant are word processing, book keeping, communications with customers and clients alike.

Management of clients and campaigns is also another area that can be managed by a virtual assistant. All these are choices that the individual would need to decide on in terms of what is going to be offered to the client as part of the services rendered.

Once the decision is made as to the type of services that is going to be offered by the virtual assistant then the necessary skills and tools should also be available for the smooth running of the contract given.

In most cases there will be a need to market the virtual assistant's skills to create the platform for interested parties and clients to consider. This marketing exercise can be done online as the exposure for the virtual assistant can be unlimited and borderless.

# Chapter 5:

*Know Your Budget*

---

# Synopsis

Comparatively the virtual assistant business required a much smaller budget than other styles of business. However this does not mean that there should not be some serious thought given to the budgeting exercise. Taking the time to think through all the necessary elements that will contribute to the success of the business will help the individual design a suitable and workable budget.

# The Money

The following are some tips on what and how to plan the budget for the success of the virtual assistant business:

The budgeting exercise should ideally take into account all operational cost needed to sustain the business for at least 12 months.

This time frame will give the individual a chance to get the business up and running and bringing in some revenue without having to worry about the immediate costs of the business entity.

Since the virtual business style is mainly conducted through online platforms, the individual should be well versed with the various computer programs available for use, thus choosing some of these tools to assist in the set up of the operations of the business may help to keep the budgeting cost lower.

With a set budget in place, the individual will have a better picture of the freedom and constraints he or she will have to work around. This will help especially when it comes to acquiring the equipment suitable for sustaining the business engine.

It will also help in decision for future expansion and maybe even the hiring of staff when and if needed.

Understating the importance of having a budget will also help the individual considering the virtual assistance type of business, get a better picture of the profits margins that can be enjoyed or whether the business in a viable enough one to venture into. Armed with this information better calculated decisions can be made.

# Chapter 6:

*Have A Business Plan*

---

# Synopsis

Having a business plan clearly drawn up not only helps the individual to have an overview of the hoped business endeavor but to also give the individual a sense of direction to be followed in order to see the business to its success anticipated state.

# Put The Plan Together

The following are some tips on how to start a business plan for the virtual assistance business:

The business overview is an important motivational piece of information that will help to keep the focus of the individual on the business at hand. This overview will also help the individual and others connected to the business, have goals clearly in place to work towards.

Having all the necessary products and services intended to be offered should also be included in the business plan. Clearly defining these elements will also help direct the individual when taking on assignments for its suitability and convenience.

If will also provide information for future reference should there be a need for expansion or redesigning of the business direction.

The business plan should include element such as the marketing strategy to be adopted for the realization of the business successes projected. In order to design a suitable marketing strategy, relevant issues such as discussions on products and service pricing should be decided upon thus giving a clear picture of what will be extended to the future client base.

Advertising campaign and how extensive or simple should also be decided and noted in the business plan.

The initial stages may require a little more commitment to the advertising side of the business as there is a need to create visibility for the business.

This particular addition to the business plan is mostly instrumental in keeping the business owner from getting carried away with the enthusiasm of creating visibility for the business.

# Chapter 7:

*Using Sites Like Scriptlance To Find Clients*

# Synopsis

When deciding to venture into the business field for one's self there is a lot of factors to consider, to ensure mistakes and misconceptions are kept to a minimal. Therefore in doing so it may be a wise thing to practice sourcing for information, comments, success stories, assisting tools and other beneficial elements that may help make the business planning easier and the customer search more fruitful.

# Finding Business

There are a lot of sites on the internet that can help the individual promote his or her business endeavor and some of these sites provide more beneficial assistance than others.

However the important thing for the business owner to do is to identify exactly what is the purpose of accessing such sights to begin with.

Then this purpose is clearly identified then the relevant searches and matches can be done. There are sites that will help to connect potential customers to the merchants and likewise there are sites that provide information and discussions on the topics relevant to the business owner's search.

Some of the sites on the internet will provide these services for a small onetime fee, while there are others that require the individual to sign on as a member and yet others which provide help in an exchange style setting.

Here too there is a need for the individual to carefully consider the merits of each site for its suitability and compatibility to the needs of the intended business endeavor.

Without this careful consideration there can be very real problems of signing on for something that does not really benefit and even worse cause a lot of headaches for the new business owner.

The main idea of creating a links to such choices made is to ensure the higher possibility of visibility for the business endeavor, and through this visibility it is hoped that the business entity will be able to garner the types and amounts of assignments that will eventually contribute to a successful business entity.

# Chapter 8:



---

# Synopsis

The following are some reasons as to why the marketing for clients is important to ensuring they keep coming back:

# Marketing

Although it may seem strange for the visual assistant to be garnering customers for the clients, if argued from a business angle, it would ideally mean more income for the virtual assistant when the client require his or her services for the new accounts.

This of course would be an ideal situation both for the virtual assistance and the original client and prove to be a rather strong liaison for the future.

Due to the nature of the virtual assistant's exposure to the client and customer base, helping to market the client's company will be much easier to do as the individual will already be very familiar with all the capabilities of the company and can vouch for its credibility.

This is also possible to further promote, as the virtual assistant will actually be promoting the company by assuring the customer that some of the work will actually be done by the assistant himself or herself.

If the customer is familiar with the virtual assistance work ethics and performance levels this particular promotional platform may bring about a positive commitment of the part of the customer.

By helping to promote the client's business, the virtual assistant is also creating a loyalty bond with the client whereby the client would be hard pressed not to give contracts to the said virtual assistance due to the help extended.

# Chapter 9:

*Handling Clients Correctly*

---

# Synopsis

Part of creating a successful business lies in the ability to handle clients well. Understanding their various need and quirks will help the virtual assistant tailor approaching styles on handling the clients effectively and beneficially. Not all clients are alike and knowing how to adjust to accommodate the various types will eventually bring about phenomenal successes and less stress.

# Doing It Right

The following are some of the tips of how to recognize categorized clients and the suitable corresponding ways of handling them:

When a client seems disorientated with the jargon dominant speech, it is time to change the content of the verbal approach or presentation.

Failing to ensure this may cause the client to eventually decide to go with a competitor, who is more attuned to the lack of technical knowledge of the client.

Not all clients are willing to declare their inaptness toward the technical aspect of the business entity, thus by not being sensitive to this the virtual assistant risks losing the client altogether.

Some clients may display disinterest in what the virtual assistant is trying to sell, mainly due to the budget constraints of the client. There are two ways the virtual assistant can handle such situations and these may include looking elsewhere for clients or trying to redesign a different package to accommodate the client's budget.

The former choice would only be feasible if the said client's budget is too small for consideration against the workload put in by the virtual assistant.

There are also some clients who seem to want to extend the hands on approach. While this can be very distracting and destructive to a certain extent, the diplomacy extended by the virtual assistant in handling such a client would be the deciding factor on the client retaining the services of the assistant. The practice of diplomacy would require some patience and persuasive qualities to be mastered.

# Wrapping Up

Having a healthy client base is the point of the entire business existence because without this healthy client base there really is no business to speak of. A healthy client base is also what is going to generate the income projected to keep the business entity successful and visible, thus facilitating future expansion possibilities.

www.ingramcontent.com/pod-product-compliance
Lightning Source LLC
LaVergne TN
LVHW041257200726
843507LV00013B/3021